High-Tech Bushcraft: ' Guide Blending Traditional Skills with Modern Technology

Master Classic Bushcraft While Leveraging Cutting-Edge Tools for Survival

CONTENTS:

Introduction

- What is High-Tech Bushcraft? (Traditional survival meets modern innovation)
- Why Blend Classic and Modern Survival Techniques?
- Who is This Guide For? (Preppers, adventurers, hikers, off-grid enthusiasts)

Chapter 1: Bushcraft Basics - The Foundation of Survival

- Understanding the Core Principles of Bushcraft (Shelter, Fire, Water, Food, Navigation)
- Essential Gear: What Every Survivalist Needs
- Traditional vs. Modern Survival Approaches

Chapter 2: Shelter & Smart Gear Innovations

- Building Traditional Shelters: Lean-to, Debris Hut, A-Frame
- Modern Shelter Options: Lightweight Tents, Bivy Bags, and Emergency Blankets
- Smart Survival Clothing: Heated Jackets, Moisture-Wicking Layers, and UV Protection

Chapter 3: Fire-Making Techniques - Old and New

- Traditional Fire-Starting Methods (Flint & Steel, Bow Drill, Fire Plough)
- Modern Fire Solutions (Plasma Lighters, Fire-Starting Gels, Solar Fire Starters)
- Best Firewood & Weatherproof Fire Tips

Chapter 4: Water Purification - From Primitive to High-Tech

- Finding Water in the Wild: Streams, Plants, and Condensation
- Traditional Purification Methods (Boiling, Charcoal Filtration)
- Modern Water Filtration & Purifiers (LifeStraw, UV Sterilizers, Reverse Osmosis Bottles)

Chapter 5: High-Tech Navigation & Tracking

- Using the Sun, Stars, and Landmarks

- Compasses vs. GPS: When to Use Which
- Best Survival Navigation Apps (Gaia GPS, AllTrails, etc.)
- Drones for Scouting & Safety (Best Models & How to Use Them in the Wild)

Chapter 6: Food & Foraging in the Digital Age

- Wild Edibles Identification: Traditional Knowledge
- Foraging Apps & AI-Powered Plant Identification
- Hunting & Fishing Gadgets: Thermal Scopes, Fish Finders, and More
- DIY Survival Food: Freeze-Drying, Solar Dehydration, and Smart Preservation

Chapter 7: Modern Survival Tools & Emergency Tech

- Best Multi-Tools & Smart Knives
- Solar Chargers & Power Banks for Off-Grid Energy
- Ham Radios, Satellite Phones & Emergency Beacons
- 3D-Printed Survival Tools: Customizing Your Own Gear

Chapter 8: Self-Defense & Security in the Wild

- Traditional Self-Defense: Spears, Traps, and Primitive Weapons
- Modern Survival Weapons: Compact Crossbows, Tactical Pens, and Pepper Spray

- Best Motion Sensors & Perimeter Alarms for Campsites

Chapter 9: Medical Preparedness - Traditional & Tech-Driven

- Basic Wilderness First Aid Skills
- Survival First Aid Kits: What to Pack
- Smart Health Gadgets: Heart Rate Monitors, Portable ECGs, and AI-Driven Health Apps
- Using Drones for Medical Supplies Delivery in Remote Areas

Chapter 10: Off-Grid Living & Long-Term Survival

- Setting Up a High-Tech Off-Grid Base
- Solar & Wind Energy for Sustainable Survival
- Building a Bushcraft Smart Home with Rainwater Collection & Hydroponics
- Best Survival Communities & Online Networks

Final Thoughts & Bonus Resources

- Checklist: High-Tech vs. Traditional Bushcraft Essentials
- Best Websites, Apps, and Tools for Survivalists
- Recommended Bushcraft YouTubers, Podcasts & Experts to Follow
- Printable Emergency Survival Cheat Sheet

High-Tech Bushcraft: The Ultimate Survival Guide Blending Traditional Skills with Modern Technology

Master Classic Bushcraft While Leveraging Cutting-Edge Tools for Survival

Introduction

What is High-Tech Bushcraft?

Bushcraft is the art of living and thriving in the wilderness using natural resources, primitive skills, and survival knowledge passed down for generations. Traditional bushcraft relies on fire-making, shelter-building, foraging, tracking, and other essential outdoor skills that enable a person to survive and adapt in nature. However, as technology advances, a new branch of survivalism has emerged—one that integrates modern innovations with time-tested wilderness techniques. This fusion is what we call *High-Tech Bushcraft*.

High-Tech Bushcraft is the perfect marriage between classic survival skills and cutting-edge tools. It is not about replacing traditional knowledge but enhancing it with modern equipment, techniques, and scientific advancements. Whether it's using solar-powered gadgets to charge essential devices, deploying satellite communication systems for emergency contact, or utilizing advanced water purification methods, High-Tech Bushcraft ensures that you are equipped with both ancient wisdom and the latest innovations to maximize your chances of survival.

Why Blend Classic and Modern Survival Techniques?

Survivalists, outdoor enthusiasts, and preppers have long debated the balance between traditional and modern techniques. While some purists argue that true survival is about mastering ancient skills without reliance on technology, others embrace the fact that human progress has provided us with remarkable tools that can significantly increase our odds of survival. High-Tech Bushcraft seeks to harmonize these two schools of thought for the following reasons:

1. Redundancy Increases Survival Odds

One of the cardinal rules of survival is redundancy—having multiple ways to achieve the same goal. While knowing how to start a fire with a bow drill is invaluable, having a ferrocerium rod or a plasma arc lighter as a backup ensures you can generate fire under any circumstances. Similarly, carrying an ultralight tarp doesn't negate the importance of knowing how to build a debris shelter, but it provides an efficient and reliable alternative when time and resources are limited.

2. Enhancing Efficiency and Energy Conservation

Traditional bushcraft methods often require significant effort and energy. A survivalist might spend hours fashioning primitive tools, whereas modern gear can accomplish the same tasks in minutes. For example, a high-tech water filter can instantly purify drinking water, saving valuable time and reducing the risk of dehydration compared to boiling or using traditional filtration methods like charcoal and sand.

3. Access to Advanced Safety and Communication

One of the greatest advantages of incorporating modern technology into bushcraft is the ability to stay connected and call for help in emergencies. GPS devices, satellite messengers, and emergency beacons provide lifelines that our ancestors never had. While knowing how to navigate using the sun and stars is a crucial skill, having a GPS backup ensures you won't get lost in unfamiliar terrain.

4. Preparedness for a Wide Range of Scenarios

Nature is unpredictable, and survival situations vary widely. A combination of old and new techniques ensures you are prepared for diverse challenges. For example, knowledge of edible wild plants is essential for long-term sustenance, but carrying a compact freeze-dried food supply can prevent immediate starvation. Similarly, while setting snares and traps is useful, having an ultralight fishing kit or a collapsible hunting bow increases your chances of securing food.

5. Adaptation to Changing Environments

Climate change and human encroachment have altered natural landscapes, making some traditional survival strategies less effective. Advanced weather prediction apps, lightweight synthetic insulation materials, and portable solar power sources allow modern survivalists to adapt more effectively to extreme conditions, whether in the Arctic, desert, or rainforest.

Who is This Guide For?

High-Tech Bushcraft is designed for anyone who wants to master survival in the modern age while respecting and utilizing time-honored techniques. This guide caters to a variety of individuals, including:

1. Preppers and Survivalists

Preppers seek to be ready for any emergency, from economic collapse to natural disasters. They understand the value of both self-reliance and technological advantages. This guide will teach them how to combine traditional survival methods with high-tech tools to create a well-rounded preparedness plan.

2. Adventurers and Explorers

Hikers, campers, and backcountry explorers often venture into remote areas where modern comforts are unavailable. By blending classic bushcraft with modern tools, they can enhance safety, efficiency, and enjoyment during their expeditions.

3. Off-Grid Enthusiasts and Homesteaders

Those who choose to live off-grid or pursue a self-sufficient lifestyle benefit greatly from High-Tech Bushcraft. Whether using renewable energy sources, modern food preservation techniques, or advanced first-aid supplies, this guide will help them optimize their survival strategies.

4. Military Personnel and Tactical Operators

Members of the military, law enforcement, and search-and-rescue teams require advanced survival skills in extreme environments. By incorporating both traditional and high-tech survival methods, they can improve their effectiveness and resilience in the field.

5. Beginners and Urban Dwellers Seeking Emergency Preparedness

Even those with little outdoor experience can benefit from this guide. In an emergency, urban dwellers may need to evacuate cities and survive in the wild. Learning fundamental bushcraft skills alongside modern survival technology ensures they are prepared for the unexpected.

Conclusion

High-Tech Bushcraft is about embracing the best of both worlds. Traditional survival skills provide the foundation for self-reliance, while modern technology enhances efficiency, safety, and adaptability. This guide will walk you through mastering both disciplines, ensuring that you are fully prepared for any survival scenario—whether in the deep wilderness, a natural disaster, or an off-grid lifestyle.

Chapter 1: Bushcraft Basics - The Foundation of Survival

Understanding the Core Principles of Bushcraft

Bushcraft is the art of living in harmony with nature, utilizing natural resources for survival and self-sufficiency. It is built on five fundamental principles:

1. Shelter

A proper shelter protects against the elements, maintains body temperature, and provides a safe resting space. The type of shelter depends on location, weather, and available materials. Examples include:

- **Lean-To Shelter** – A simple structure using a ridgepole and natural materials.
- **Debris Hut** – A fully enclosed shelter ideal for cold environments.
- **Tarp and Hammock Setup** – Lightweight and effective for quick deployment.

2. Fire

Fire is essential for warmth, cooking, signaling, and protection. There are multiple methods to create fire:

- **Friction-Based Methods** – Bow drill, hand drill, fire plow.
- **Flint and Steel** – Striking steel against flint or quartz to generate sparks.
- **Ferrocerium Rod** – A modern fire-starting tool that produces hot sparks.
- **Fire Lays** – Different configurations such as teepee, log cabin, and Dakota fire hole to optimize fire efficiency.

3. Water

Securing clean water is a survival priority. Techniques include:

- **Finding Water Sources** – Streams, rivers, rainwater, and underground sources.
- **Purification Methods** – Boiling, filtering, and chemical purification.

- **Solar Still and Condensation Traps** – Passive water collection techniques.

4. Food

Foraging, hunting, and fishing provide essential nutrients. Key sources include:

- **Edible Plants and Wild Greens** – Berries, roots, and nuts.
- **Trapping and Hunting** – Small game snares, fishing lines, and bows.
- **Insects and Alternative Protein Sources** – High-protein survival food.

5. Navigation

Navigation ensures safe travel and location awareness. Techniques include:

- **Natural Navigation** – Using the sun, stars, and natural landmarks.
- **Compass and Map Reading** – Understanding topographic maps and bearings.

- **Dead Reckoning** – Estimating distance and direction traveled.

Essential Gear: What Every Survivalist Needs

Having the right gear can mean the difference between life and death. Key survival items include:

- **Cutting Tools** – Fixed-blade knife, folding knife, and saw.
- **Fire-Starting Equipment** – Ferro rods, waterproof matches, lighters.
- **Shelter Supplies** – Tarp, emergency bivvy, paracord.
- **Water Purification Tools** – Portable filters, purification tablets, canteens.
- **Navigation Aids** – Compass, topographic maps, GPS device.
- **First Aid Kit** – Bandages, antiseptic, pain relievers, emergency medications.
- **Signaling Devices** – Whistle, mirror, flashlight.

- **Food Gathering Tools** – Fishing kit, snares, slingshot.

Choosing durable, multi-purpose gear maximizes efficiency and preparedness in any survival scenario.

Traditional vs. Modern Survival Approaches

Traditional Bushcraft

Traditional bushcraft relies on ancestral knowledge, primitive tools, and nature-based techniques. It emphasizes:

- **Minimalism** – Using natural materials instead of manufactured gear.
- **Handcrafted Tools** – Making fire, shelters, and hunting weapons from raw materials.
- **Adaptability** – Learning through direct experience and deep observation of nature.

Modern Survivalism

Modern survivalism integrates advanced tools, technology, and scientific knowledge for improved efficiency. It includes:

- **Synthetic Materials** – Lightweight and durable gear like Mylar blankets and Kevlar cordage.
- **High-Tech Navigation** – GPS devices, satellite communication tools.
- **Emergency Preparedness** – Stockpiling food, first aid kits, and survival manuals.

Which is Better?

Both approaches have advantages. Traditional bushcraft fosters deep connection with nature and long-term survival skills, while modern survivalism ensures immediate safety and efficiency. A balanced survivalist blends both methods for maximum preparedness.

Conclusion

Mastering the fundamentals of bushcraft builds confidence and self-reliance in any environment. Whether embracing ancestral skills or modern tools, the key to survival is knowledge, adaptability, and resourcefulness. In the following chapters, we will explore each principle in greater detail, equipping you with the skills necessary to thrive in the wild.

Chapter 2: Shelter & Smart Gear Innovations

Survival in the wilderness or extreme conditions requires not only knowledge of traditional shelter-building techniques but also an understanding of modern innovations in shelter and survival gear. This chapter explores both time-tested and cutting-edge approaches to staying warm, dry, and safe in the outdoors.

Building Traditional Shelters

When stranded or navigating remote areas, knowing how to construct a traditional shelter can be a lifesaving skill. Here are three essential types of natural shelters:

Lean-to Shelter

A **lean-to shelter** is one of the simplest and most effective survival structures. It requires minimal resources and provides protection against wind and rain.

How to Build:

1. Find a strong, horizontal support beam (such as a thick branch) and secure it between two trees or other sturdy supports.
2. Lean long branches or poles at an angle against the support beam, forming a sloped roof.
3. Cover the slanted surface with leaves, pine needles, or bark to provide insulation and waterproofing.
4. Position the open side away from the wind to reduce exposure.

Best for: Mild conditions, wind protection, quick assembly.

Debris Hut

A **debris hut** is a fully enclosed structure that offers excellent insulation, ideal for cold environments.

How to Build:

1. Construct a frame by leaning branches against a central support beam, forming an A-frame shape.

2. Weave smaller branches into the frame for stability.
3. Pile leaves, moss, and other debris over the structure to create thick insulation.
4. Ensure a small opening for entrance while keeping the interior compact to retain body heat.

Best for: Cold climates, extended survival, full-body coverage.

A-Frame Shelter

The **A-frame shelter** is similar to the debris hut but offers more space and stability.

How to Build:

1. Form two angled walls by leaning branches on opposite sides of a central ridgepole.
2. Secure the structure with cross-bracing and add layers of insulation like foliage or a tarp.
3. Close off one side if additional wind protection is needed.

Best for: Long-term shelter, better protection from rain and wind, adaptable design.

Modern Shelter Options

For those who prefer pre-made solutions, modern shelter innovations offer convenience, portability, and enhanced protection against the elements.

Lightweight Tents

Modern lightweight tents are designed for easy transport while providing robust shelter in a variety of conditions. Key features include:

- **Waterproof and wind-resistant materials** to withstand storms.
- **Freestanding and quick setup designs** for convenience.
- **Ultralight materials** such as silnylon or Dyneema for minimal weight.

Best for: Backpackers, extreme weather conditions, long-term outdoor stays.

Bivy Bags: A **bivy bag** (short for bivouac sack) is a minimalist shelter alternative to a tent.

Advantages:

- Compact and lightweight, perfect for ultralight hiking or emergency use.
- Offers **waterproof and breathable** protection.
- Works as an emergency backup if a full tent is not an option.

Best for: Solo adventurers, emergency shelter, minimalists.

Emergency Blankets

Emergency blankets (or space blankets) are made of **heat-reflective material** designed to retain body heat.

Uses:

- Wrap around the body for warmth.
- Create a makeshift shelter by tying it between trees.
- Signal for rescue with its reflective surface.

Best for: Hypothermia prevention, emergency situations, compact survival kits.

Smart Survival Clothing

In addition to shelter, wearing the right gear can mean the difference between comfort and extreme hardship. Modern survival clothing incorporates advanced technology to regulate body temperature, wick moisture, and protect against environmental hazards.

Heated Jackets

Battery-powered **heated jackets** are a game-changer for cold-weather survival.

Features:

- Carbon fiber or graphene-based heating elements distribute warmth across the torso.
- Rechargeable batteries last for hours, providing sustained heat.
- Multiple heat settings allow for temperature control.

Best for: Extreme cold, winter hiking, outdoor work.

Moisture-Wicking Layers

Moisture control is critical in survival situations, as wet clothing can lead to hypothermia.

Types of moisture-wicking layers:

- **Base layers:** Made of merino wool or synthetic fibers to pull sweat away from the skin.
- **Mid-layers:** Fleece or down insulation to retain warmth.
- **Outer layers:** Waterproof and breathable shells to protect against rain and wind.

Best for: All-weather survival, active movement in the wild.

UV Protection Clothing

Long exposure to the sun, especially in deserts or high-altitude areas, requires **UV-resistant clothing** to prevent burns and skin damage.

Key benefits:

- **UPF-rated fabrics** block harmful UV rays.

- Lightweight and breathable materials provide comfort.
- Some designs incorporate insect repellent treatments for extra protection.

Best for: Hot climates, desert survival, high-altitude trekking.

Conclusion

Whether relying on traditional survival skills or embracing modern innovations, understanding shelter and smart gear technology is essential for outdoor survival. By mastering basic shelter-building techniques and incorporating advanced clothing and equipment, you can be better prepared to face any environment. Adaptability is key—combining knowledge of both primitive and high-tech solutions ensures a well-rounded approach to staying safe in the wild.

Chapter 3: Fire-Making Techniques - Old and New

Fire is one of humanity's most essential survival tools, providing warmth, cooking capabilities, and protection. Throughout history, various methods have been developed to create fire, ranging from ancient friction-based techniques to modern technological solutions. This chapter explores traditional and modern fire-starting methods and offers insights into selecting the best firewood and weatherproofing your fire.

Traditional Fire-Starting Methods

Before the advent of matches and lighters, our ancestors relied on manual fire-starting techniques. These methods require skill and patience but can be invaluable in survival situations.

1. Flint & Steel

One of the oldest fire-starting techniques, flint and steel involve striking a piece of high-carbon steel against flint or quartz to produce sparks. These sparks land on a charred cloth or dry tinder, which is then nurtured into a flame.

- **Pros:** Reliable, reusable, works in damp conditions
- **Cons:** Requires proper technique, needs dry tinder

2. Bow Drill

The bow drill is a friction-based fire-starting method that uses a spindle, a bow, a socket, and a fireboard. The bow moves the spindle rapidly against the fireboard, creating heat through friction and eventually forming an ember.

- **Pros:** Does not require metal, works with natural materials
- **Cons:** Physically demanding, requires practice and dry wood

3. Fire Plough

This technique involves rubbing a hardwood stick along a groove in a softer fireboard. The repeated motion generates enough heat to create an ember.

- **Pros:** Simple materials required
- **Cons:** Requires significant effort, less effective in damp conditions

Modern Fire Solutions

Technology has revolutionized fire-making, offering easy and reliable ways to start fires with minimal effort. Here are some of the most effective modern fire-starting tools.

1. Plasma Lighters

Plasma lighters use electricity to generate an arc of high-intensity heat capable of igniting paper, dry grass, or other fine tinder. They are rechargeable and windproof, making them an excellent survival tool.

- **Pros:** Works in any weather, reusable, no fuel needed
- **Cons:** Requires charging, not suitable for larger wood pieces directly

2. Fire-Starting Gels & Cubes

These chemical-based fire starters are designed to ignite instantly and burn for extended periods. They are ideal for lighting wet wood or creating a fire quickly in adverse conditions.

- **Pros:** Long burn time, reliable in all conditions
- **Cons:** Single-use, requires storage

3. Solar Fire Starters

Solar fire starters use magnification to focus sunlight on tinder, eventually generating enough heat to create an ember. They are lightweight and work well in sunny environments.

- **Pros:** Unlimited use, no fuel required
- **Cons:** Ineffective in cloudy or nighttime conditions

Best Firewood & Weatherproof Fire Tips

Choosing the right firewood and knowing how to weatherproof your fire can make all the difference, especially in survival situations.

Best Firewood Types

Hardwoods burn hotter and longer, making them ideal for sustaining a fire.

- **Best Choices:** Oak, hickory, maple, beech, ash
- **Avoid:** Greenwood, pine, or other resinous woods, which produce excessive smoke and burn inefficiently

Weatherproof Fire Tips

1. **Use Dry Tinder and Kindling:** Store tinder (such as dry leaves, bark shavings, or cotton balls) in waterproof containers.

2. **Wind Protection:** Build a small windbreak with rocks or logs to shield the flame from strong gusts.
3. **Fire Structure:** In wet conditions, use the *teepee* or *log cabin* structure to maximize airflow and keep the inner core dry.
4. **Waterproof Fire Starter Kit:** Keep waterproof matches, a ferrocerium rod, or a plasma lighter as backups.
5. **Elevate Fire on Wet Ground:** Build a base of dry wood or bark to keep the fire off damp surfaces.

Mastering fire-making techniques ensures you can always create warmth and light when needed, whether you rely on ancient skills or modern tools. With the right knowledge, you'll be prepared for any survival situation or outdoor adventure.

Chapter 4: Water Purification - From Primitive to High-Tech

Finding Water in the Wild: Streams, Plants, and Condensation

Water is the most crucial element for survival. Without it, the human body can only last a few days before dehydration sets in. When stranded in the wild, finding water should be a top priority. Here are several natural sources and techniques for locating water:

Streams and Rivers

Flowing water is often safer to drink than stagnant water, as it is less likely to harbor bacteria, parasites, and contaminants. However, even clear-looking water may contain harmful microorganisms, so purification is necessary. Look for small streams, especially in valleys or areas where vegetation is lush, as these indicate the presence of water.

Rainwater Collection

Rainwater is one of the safest natural water sources. You can collect it using large leaves, tarps, or any concave surface. If you have a plastic sheet, you can funnel rainwater into a container for later use.

Dew and Condensation

In dry environments, morning dew can be an important water source. You can collect it by tying an absorbent cloth around your ankles and walking through tall grass early in the morning. Wring out the cloth to retrieve the collected moisture. Additionally, condensation can be captured by creating a solar still—digging a hole, placing vegetation inside, and covering it with plastic to trap evaporated water.

Plant-Based Water Sources

Certain plants store drinkable water. Cacti, bamboo, and vines often contain liquid that can be extracted. Coconut trees provide both drinkable coconut water and moisture-rich flesh. Additionally, digging near the base of trees or in dry riverbeds may reveal underground water sources.

Traditional Purification Methods (Boiling, Charcoal Filtration)

Once water is collected, it must be purified to remove bacteria, viruses, parasites, and debris. Traditional purification methods have been used for centuries and remain reliable today.

Boiling Water

Boiling is one of the most effective ways to kill harmful microorganisms in water. To properly purify water by boiling:

1. Bring the water to a rolling boil.
2. Maintain the boil for at least one minute (or three minutes at altitudes above 6,500 feet / 2,000 meters).
3. Allow the water to cool before drinking.

Charcoal Filtration

A simple and effective method of removing impurities is through charcoal filtration. To make a primitive charcoal filter:

1. Collect charcoal from a campfire and crush it into small pieces.
2. Layer the charcoal between sand and small pebbles in a container or cloth.
3. Pour the water through the filter multiple times to remove dirt and some toxins.
4. Follow up with boiling to ensure microbial safety.

Solar Disinfection (SODIS)

Solar disinfection involves using UV radiation to kill pathogens. Simply fill a clear plastic bottle with water and leave it in direct sunlight for 6-8 hours. This method is particularly useful in emergencies when no fire or filtration system is available.

Modern Water Filtration & Purifiers

Advancements in technology have led to highly effective and portable water purification solutions. These tools are especially valuable for hikers, survivalists, and travelers.

LifeStraw

LifeStraw is a compact, straw-like device that allows users to drink directly from contaminated water sources. It uses a hollow fiber membrane that filters out bacteria, parasites, and microplastics. However, it does not remove viruses or chemical contaminants.

UV Sterilizers

UV purifiers, such as the SteriPEN, use ultraviolet light to destroy microorganisms at a DNA level. To use:

1. Fill a bottle with clear water.
2. Insert the UV device and stir for the recommended time (usually 60-90 seconds).

3. Once complete, the water is safe to drink.

This method is highly effective but requires a power source (batteries or USB charging) and works best in clear water.

Reverse Osmosis Bottles

Reverse osmosis (RO) is one of the most advanced filtration methods available. RO purifiers use a semi-permeable membrane to remove:

- Bacteria
- Viruses
- Heavy metals
- Salts
- Chemicals

These bottles are excellent for travel, but they require pressure (manual pumping or gravity-based systems) to push water through the membrane. Some models also incorporate carbon filters to improve taste and remove additional contaminants.

Conclusion

From ancient methods like boiling and charcoal filtration to high-tech solutions like LifeStraw and reverse osmosis bottles, water purification has evolved dramatically. Whether you are in the wild or preparing for emergencies, understanding these techniques ensures safe hydration in any environment. Adopting the right method depends on available resources, the level of contamination, and the desired convenience. Ultimately, clean water is essential for survival, and knowing how to obtain it can make all the difference.

Chapter 5: High-Tech Navigation & Tracking

Survival and exploration rely on the ability to navigate effectively. Whether using traditional celestial navigation, modern GPS systems, or drones for scouting and safety, understanding different techniques can mean the difference between staying on track and getting lost. In this chapter, we explore various navigation methods and how to integrate high-tech solutions with traditional survival techniques.

Using the Sun, Stars, and Landmarks

Before GPS and digital maps, explorers, sailors, and survivalists used natural indicators to find their way. While technology has advanced, these traditional methods remain valuable, especially when electronic devices fail due to battery depletion, signal loss, or environmental conditions.

The Sun

- The sun rises in the east and sets in the west. By noting its movement, you can approximate cardinal directions.
- At noon, the sun is at its highest point in the sky in the northern hemisphere, pointing south, and vice versa in the southern hemisphere.
- A stick-and-shadow method can be used to determine east-west by tracking the shortest shadow over time.

The Stars

- The North Star (Polaris) remains almost stationary in the northern sky and indicates true north.
- The Southern Cross constellation helps determine south in the southern hemisphere.
- Stars and their movement patterns can serve as navigational aids on clear nights.

Landmarks

- Mountains, rivers, and valleys provide natural indicators of direction.
- Man-made structures such as towers, roads, and power lines can be used as reference points.
- Following a river downstream often leads to settlements or roads.

Compasses vs. GPS: When to Use Which

Both traditional compasses and GPS devices have their place in navigation. Understanding their strengths and weaknesses can help you decide when to rely on each.

Compass Navigation

- Works without batteries or satellite signals.
- Provides a consistent sense of direction regardless of weather conditions.
- Best for dense forests, caves, or deep valleys where GPS signals might be weak.

- Requires knowledge of topographic maps for effective use.

GPS Navigation

- Offers real-time positioning with precise latitude and longitude coordinates.
- Provides detailed maps, elevation data, and route tracking.
- Useful for urban environments, open terrain, and planned hikes.
- Susceptible to battery drain, satellite obstructions, and signal loss in remote areas.

When to Use Which?

- Use a compass as a backup when GPS fails.
- Rely on GPS for convenience and real-time tracking.
- Combine both tools for redundancy and safety.

Best Survival Navigation Apps

Modern smartphones and handheld GPS devices have revolutionized outdoor navigation. Here are some of the best survival navigation apps available:

Gaia GPS

- Offers detailed topographic and satellite maps.
- Allows offline map downloads for remote locations.
- Ideal for hikers, backpackers, and survivalists.

AllTrails

- Provides trail maps with user reviews and difficulty ratings.
- Tracks progress and suggests alternate routes.
- Great for casual hikers and adventurers.

Google Maps (Offline Mode)

- Allows downloading of maps for use without an internet connection.
- Offers road navigation, points of interest, and terrain views.
- Limited in deep wilderness settings.

ViewRanger

- Includes augmented reality for identifying peaks and landmarks.
- Offers GPS tracking with detailed maps.
- Useful for mountaineers and off-trail explorers.

onX Hunt

- Designed for hunters but useful for general navigation.
- Features private and public land boundaries.
- Includes offline maps and waypoint marking.

Tips for Using Navigation Apps Effectively:

- Always carry a power bank or solar charger.
- Download offline maps before entering remote areas.
- Learn how to read topographic maps to supplement digital tools.

Drones for Scouting & Safety

Drones have become an essential tool for explorers, search-and-rescue teams, and survivalists. They provide aerial views of terrain, helping with route planning and detecting obstacles. Here's how to use them effectively in the wild:

Best Drone Models for Navigation & Safety

1. **DJI Mavic 3** – Long battery life, excellent camera, and obstacle avoidance.
2. **Autel Robotics EVO II** – High-resolution camera, rugged design, and thermal imaging options.
3. **DJI Mini 3 Pro** – Compact and lightweight, ideal for quick aerial scouting.
4. **Parrot Anafi USA** – Military-grade durability, thermal sensors, and great zoom capabilities.

How to Use Drones in the Wild

- **Scouting Ahead**: Fly a drone to check the terrain, identify obstacles, and find water sources or safe routes.
- **Search and Rescue**: Use drones with thermal imaging to locate missing people or animals.

- **Emergency Signaling**: Some drones can carry LED lights or sound alarms to attract attention.
- **Wildlife Monitoring**: Observe dangerous animals from a safe distance.

Drone Usage Tips

- Ensure compliance with local laws and regulations.
- Carry extra batteries and a portable charger.
- Avoid flying in extreme weather conditions.
- Keep drones within visual line of sight.

Conclusion

Mastering both traditional and high-tech navigation tools ensures you're prepared for any environment. By combining celestial navigation, compasses, GPS devices, survival apps, and drones, you can significantly improve your ability to navigate, track progress, and ensure safety. Whether exploring the wilderness, engaging in search-and-rescue missions, or preparing for emergencies, these techniques will enhance your survival skills and confidence in the wild.

Chapter 6: Food & Foraging in the Digital Age

The way humans gather and preserve food has evolved significantly with the integration of modern technology. While traditional foraging, hunting, and food preservation methods remain valuable, the digital age has introduced powerful tools that enhance efficiency, accuracy, and sustainability. This chapter explores the intersection of ancient wisdom and modern innovation in food gathering and preservation.

Wild Edibles Identification: Traditional Knowledge

Foraging for wild edibles has been practiced for thousands of years, with indigenous and rural communities passing down extensive knowledge about which plants are safe to eat and which should be avoided. This knowledge includes:

- **Edible plant identification:** Recognizing leaves, flowers, and growth patterns of safe wild foods.

- **Toxic lookalikes:** Understanding which plants resemble edible ones but contain harmful compounds.
- **Seasonal harvesting:** Knowing the best time to collect wild foods for optimal nutrition.
- **Medicinal uses:** Many wild plants not only serve as food but also as remedies for various ailments.

By studying traditional foraging techniques, we can preserve valuable knowledge while integrating modern tools for better precision and safety.

Foraging Apps & AI-Powered Plant Identification

Advancements in artificial intelligence (AI) and mobile technology have revolutionized foraging. Apps like **Seek by iNaturalist**, **PictureThis**, and **PlantSnap** allow users to instantly identify plants, mushrooms, and even insects through image recognition. These tools use vast databases and machine learning to analyze visual characteristics and provide:

- **Instant identification:** Snap a photo and receive data on edibility, toxicity, and uses.
- **Location-based recommendations:** Apps use GPS data to suggest locally available wild foods.
- **Community verification:** Users can cross-check their findings with expert foragers.
- **Offline databases:** Some apps allow offline access, making them useful for deep wilderness exploration.

While AI-powered apps improve accuracy, users should always verify results using multiple sources before consuming wild plants.

Hunting & Fishing Gadgets: Thermal Scopes, Fish Finders, and More

For those who supplement their diet with hunting and fishing, modern technology provides a significant advantage. Some of the most innovative gadgets include:

Hunting Technology

- **Thermal scopes and night vision:** These devices detect heat signatures, making it easier to locate game in low-light conditions.
- **GPS-enabled tracking collars:** Used in conjunction with trained hunting dogs to track and locate prey.
- **Smart bows and rifles:** Equipped with rangefinders and ballistics calculators for precise targeting.
- **Electronic game calls:** Devices that mimic animal sounds to attract prey more effectively.

Fishing Technology

- **Fish finders:** Sonar-based devices that detect fish location, depth, and movement patterns.
- **Underwater drones:** Remote-controlled cameras that provide a live feed of underwater conditions.
- **Smart bait and lures:** Electronic lures that mimic real fish movement and even emit scents to attract catches.

- **Weather and tide tracking apps:** Software that provides real-time updates on optimal fishing conditions.

By combining these gadgets with traditional skills, hunters and fishers can increase efficiency while maintaining ethical and sustainable practices.

DIY Survival Food: Freeze-Drying, Solar Dehydration, and Smart Preservation

Long-term food storage is essential for survivalists, campers, and those who wish to reduce food waste. Modern preservation techniques offer enhanced ways to store food while maintaining nutritional value.

Freeze-Drying

Freeze-drying removes moisture from food while preserving its structure and nutrients. It has become accessible through home freeze-dryers like **Harvest Right**. Benefits include:

- **Extended shelf life:** Freeze-dried food can last 20+ years.
- **Lightweight and portable:** Ideal for emergency preparedness and backpacking.
- **Retention of nutrients and flavor:** Unlike traditional drying methods, freeze-drying keeps food tasting fresh.

Solar Dehydration

Solar dehydrators use natural sunlight to remove moisture, offering an energy-efficient way to preserve food. Key advantages include:

- **Low energy consumption:** No electricity required.
- **Simplicity:** Can be built at home using minimal materials.
- **Great for fruits, vegetables, and herbs:** Preserves food without additives.

Smart Preservation Techniques

Advancements in food storage technology include:

- **Vacuum sealing:** Removes oxygen to prevent spoilage.
- **Smart refrigerators and storage systems:** IoT-connected devices track food freshness and suggest usage based on expiration dates.
- **Fermentation revival:** Traditional methods like kimchi, sauerkraut, and miso are now enhanced with precise temperature and humidity controls.

Building a Sustainable Food Strategy

By combining traditional preservation techniques with modern technology, individuals can create a reliable, long-term food supply that is both sustainable and nutritious.

Conclusion

The digital age has transformed how we find, gather, and preserve food. While technology offers unparalleled convenience and precision, the foundation of food security still lies in traditional knowledge and sustainable practices. By integrating AI, smart devices, and advanced preservation methods with time-tested wisdom, we can create a future where food foraging and survival strategies are more effective, accessible, and resilient.

Chapter 7: Modern Survival Tools & Emergency Tech

Survival has evolved far beyond the basic tools of the past. With modern technology, survivalists, adventurers, and emergency responders now have access to high-tech gear that enhances self-sufficiency and preparedness. Whether you are preparing for natural disasters, off-grid living, or wilderness survival, integrating smart tools and emergency technology can significantly improve your chances of staying safe and connected. This chapter explores the best modern survival tools, from multi-tools to emergency communication devices and 3D-printed gear customization.

Best Multi-Tools & Smart Knives

Multi-tools have long been a staple of survival gear, but modern advancements have made them even more versatile and efficient. The latest models integrate digital features, modular designs, and durable materials to withstand extreme conditions. Here are some of the best options:

1. **Smart Multi-Tools**

- **Leatherman Free P4** – Features magnetic architecture for smooth access to tools, a one-handed opening mechanism, and 21 built-in functions.
- **Gerber Center-Drive Plus** – Designed for heavy-duty use with a full-size center-axis driver, an improved set of pliers, and a one-hand deployable knife.
- **Victorinox CyberTool M** – A multi-tool geared toward tech repair, featuring specialized bits for fixing electronic devices in emergencies.

2. **Smart Knives**

- **RAZOR Tactical Smart Knife** – A folding knife with a built-in LED flashlight, fire starter, and emergency whistle.
- **SOG Flash AT-XR** – A high-tech folding knife with an assisted opening mechanism, an

ambidextrous safety lock, and a cryogenically treated steel blade.
- **CRKT Provoke** – Features a futuristic karambit design with a rapid-deployment mechanism, perfect for self-defense and utility use.

Smart knives and multi-tools now integrate Bluetooth connectivity, allowing users to track their tools via smartphone apps. Some even have digital readouts for temperature, altitude, and barometric pressure, making them indispensable in survival situations.

Solar Chargers & Power Banks for Off-Grid Energy

Energy independence is crucial when access to the electrical grid is unavailable. The latest solar chargers and power banks provide reliable, renewable energy sources for survivalists, campers, and emergency responders.

1. Solar Chargers

- **Goal Zero Nomad 50** – A portable, foldable solar panel with USB and 12V outputs, ideal for charging devices in the wild.
- **BigBlue 28W Solar Charger** – High-efficiency solar cells that can charge multiple devices simultaneously.
- **Anker 21W PowerPort Solar** – Lightweight and weather-resistant, this charger is ideal for backpackers and survivalists needing emergency energy.

2. Power Banks

- **Jackery Explorer 500** – A robust power station capable of charging laptops, drones, and small appliances.
- **BioLite Charge 80 PD** – A compact power bank with fast-charging capabilities and a rugged, waterproof design.
- **EcoFlow River 2** – A fast-recharging portable battery with multiple AC and DC outputs.

These devices are essential for keeping GPS units, communication devices, and medical equipment powered during emergencies. Some advanced models even include hand-crank backup charging or wireless charging pads.

Ham Radios, Satellite Phones & Emergency Beacons

Communication is critical in survival situations. Whether you're dealing with natural disasters, lost in the wilderness, or off-grid for extended periods, having reliable communication tools can mean the difference between life and death.

1. Ham Radios

- **Baofeng UV-5R** – A budget-friendly, dual-band radio ideal for beginners and preppers.
- **Yaesu FT-60R** – A rugged handheld radio with a long battery life and extensive frequency range.
- **Icom IC-705** – A high-end, portable HF radio perfect for long-distance communication.

2. Satellite Phones

- **Garmin inReach Mini 2** – A compact satellite communicator with two-way messaging and SOS functionality.
- **Iridium 9555** – A global satellite phone with rugged durability and reliable voice communication.
- **Thuraya X5-Touch** – The first Android-based satellite phone with a touchscreen and dual-mode capability (satellite & GSM).

3. Emergency Beacons

- **ACR ResQLink View** – A personal locator beacon (PLB) with GPS tracking and a digital display for emergency alerts.
- **SPOT Gen4** – A satellite messenger that provides real-time tracking and SOS capabilities.
- **Ocean Signal PLB1** – The world's smallest PLB, ideal for outdoor enthusiasts and maritime emergencies.

Ham radios require licensing in many countries, but they offer a reliable communication method without dependence on cellular networks. Satellite phones and emergency beacons, on the other hand, provide global coverage and direct SOS communication with rescue services.

3D-Printed Survival Tools: Customizing Your Own Gear

3D printing has revolutionized survival gear by allowing individuals to create customized tools tailored to their specific needs. From medical devices to durable multi-use tools, 3D printing technology provides limitless possibilities for self-reliant survivalists.

1. Printable Tools & Equipment

- **Plastic and metal multi-tools** – Lightweight yet durable for small repairs and modifications.
- **Tactical gear attachments** – Custom holsters, mounts, and sheaths for knives, radios, and flashlights.
- **Medical devices** – Customized splints, tourniquets, and prosthetics in emergencies.

2. Materials for 3D-Printed Survival Gear

- **PLA+ (Polylactic Acid Plus)** – A biodegradable yet strong material for non-load-bearing tools.
- **ABS (Acrylonitrile Butadiene Styrene)** – Highly durable and impact-resistant, ideal for survival applications.
- **Nylon & Carbon Fiber Blends** – Used for ultra-strong components like knife handles and structural supports.

3. Open-Source 3D Models

Websites like Thingiverse and MyMiniFactory offer a wide selection of free, printable designs for survival tools. Many preppers and outdoor enthusiasts share designs for essential items such as:

- Fire starters
- Compass housings
- Water purification components

By utilizing 3D printing, survivalists can create tools on demand, modify existing designs for efficiency, and even print repair parts in the field using portable 3D printers.

Conclusion

Modern survival is about integrating the best of traditional knowledge with cutting-edge technology. Smart multi-tools and knives provide enhanced versatility, solar chargers and power banks ensure off-grid energy independence, ham radios and satellite phones maintain critical communication links, and 3D-printed survival tools allow for customization and adaptability. Whether preparing for emergencies, off-grid living, or adventure travel, investing in these advanced survival tools can significantly increase preparedness and resilience in any situation.

Chapter 8: Self-Defense & Security in the Wild

Surviving in the wild is not just about finding food, water, and shelter—it also involves protecting yourself from threats. These threats can range from wild animals to hostile humans, making self-defense and security a crucial aspect of wilderness survival. This chapter explores both traditional and modern self-defense techniques, as well as tools to enhance security around your campsite.

Traditional Self-Defense: Spears, Traps, and Primitive Weapons

Before the advent of firearms and modern weapons, early humans relied on ingenuity and resourcefulness to defend themselves. Many of these traditional methods remain effective today, especially in survival situations where modern weapons may not be available.

Spears

Spears are one of the oldest and most versatile weapons used for both hunting and self-defense. A properly crafted spear provides a safe distance between you and a potential threat, such as a wild animal or an intruder.

- **Materials:** Hardwoods like oak, ash, or hickory.
- **Crafting:** Sharpen the tip and harden it over fire or attach a stone/metal blade.
- **Use:** Effective for thrusting or throwing, making it ideal against both animals and attackers.

Traps

Traps are passive defense mechanisms that require little effort once set up. They are useful for both deterring threats and capturing food.

- **Deadfall Traps:** Designed to crush or immobilize intruders.
- **Snare Traps:** Useful for catching small animals but can also be scaled up for larger threats.

- **Alarm Traps:** Simple tripwire systems connected to noise-making devices to alert you of an intruder.

Primitive Weapons

- **Slingshots:** Effective for small threats and lightweight to carry.
- **Bolas:** Used to entangle legs and immobilize a target.
- **Blowguns:** Silent but effective, especially with poison-tipped darts.

Modern Survival Weapons: Compact Crossbows, Tactical Pens, and Pepper Spray

For those who prefer more contemporary solutions, modern survival weapons offer portability, efficiency, and ease of use.

Compact Crossbows

A small, lightweight crossbow can be a valuable self-defense tool. They are silent, reusable, and capable of taking down threats at a distance.

- **Advantages:** Quiet, high penetration power, and can be used for both hunting and self-defense.
- **Disadvantages:** Slower reload time compared to firearms.

Tactical Pens

A tactical pen is a disguised self-defense tool that functions as a writing instrument but can also be used as a striking weapon.

- **Features:** Made of hardened metal, often with a glass breaker tip.
- **Use:** Aim for pressure points such as the throat, eyes, or ribs.

Pepper Spray

Pepper spray is a non-lethal deterrent that can incapacitate an attacker for several minutes, allowing you to escape.

- **Effective Range:** Usually between 5-10 feet.
- **Use:** Aim for the face, particularly the eyes and nose.

- **Precautions:** Be mindful of wind direction to avoid self-contamination.

Best Motion Sensors & Perimeter Alarms for Campsites

Securing your campsite is just as important as having self-defense tools. Motion sensors and perimeter alarms provide early warnings against potential threats, giving you time to prepare or escape.

Motion Sensors

These devices detect movement and can be used to secure the perimeter of your campsite.

- **Passive Infrared (PIR) Sensors:** Detect heat signatures from living beings.
- **Ultrasonic Sensors:** Emit sound waves that bounce back to detect motion.
- **Vibration Sensors:** Detect ground movement, useful for alerting against both humans and animals.

Perimeter Alarms

Setting up a perimeter alarm can prevent unwelcome surprises during the night.

- **Tripwire Alarms:** A simple system using fishing line or paracord connected to bells or other noise-making devices.
- **Battery-Powered Alarms:** Small electronic devices that emit loud noises when triggered.
- **DIY Alarms:** Empty cans filled with rocks and suspended by strings to make noise when disturbed.

Recommended Products

1. **Wosports Motion Sensor Alarm** – A waterproof PIR motion detector with a loud alarm.
2. **Guardline Wireless Driveway Alarm** – A reliable motion sensor for campsites and remote locations.
3. **Doberman Security SE-0106** – A compact tripwire alarm with a piercing sound.

4. **SABRE Wireless Home Security Door Alarm** – Can be adapted for campsite use with a loud siren feature.

Final Thoughts

Survival is about being prepared for every situation, including self-defense. Whether using primitive tools like spears and traps or modern solutions like tactical pens and perimeter alarms, having a solid security strategy is essential. By combining these methods, you can ensure that you stay safe and protected in the wilderness.

Chapter 9: Medical Preparedness - Traditional & Tech-Driven

Basic Wilderness First Aid Skills

Survival in remote or emergency situations often depends on basic first aid knowledge. Whether hiking in the wilderness or facing an urban disaster, knowing how to administer first aid can be life-saving. Here are key skills everyone should learn:

1. **Assessing the Situation**: Quickly evaluate the scene for potential hazards and determine the best course of action.
2. **CPR and Rescue Breathing**: Cardiopulmonary resuscitation (CPR) is critical for cardiac arrest situations. Knowing how to administer chest compressions and rescue breaths can save lives.
3. **Bleeding Control**: Learn how to apply direct pressure, elevate the wound, and use a tourniquet if necessary.

4. **Fracture Stabilization**: Splinting a broken limb properly can prevent further injury and ease transport.
5. **Wound Care and Infection Prevention**: Cleaning wounds, applying antiseptics, and dressing injuries to prevent infections.
6. **Recognizing and Treating Shock**: Identify symptoms like cold skin, rapid heartbeat, and confusion, then provide appropriate care by keeping the person warm and hydrated.
7. **Handling Hypothermia and Heat Stroke**: Learn to identify symptoms and administer proper first aid, such as warming techniques or rapid cooling.

These foundational skills ensure preparedness in any survival scenario.

Survival First Aid Kits: What to Pack

A well-equipped survival first aid kit is essential for any emergency. Here's what an ideal kit should contain:

Basic Medical Supplies:

- Adhesive bandages (various sizes)
- Sterile gauze pads and adhesive tape
- Antiseptic wipes and antibiotic ointment
- Tweezers and scissors
- Thermometer
- Cotton balls and swabs

Medications:

- Pain relievers (ibuprofen, acetaminophen)
- Antihistamines (for allergic reactions)
- Anti-inflammatory drugs
- Antidiarrheal medication
- Oral rehydration salts

Advanced Supplies:

- Tourniquet
- Hemostatic agents (QuickClot, Celox)
- Splints and elastic bandages
- Sutures or butterfly closures
- N95 masks or respirators

Survival Tools:

- Emergency blanket
- Multi-tool or Swiss Army knife
- Water purification tablets
- CPR face shield
- Notepad and pen for medical records

Regularly check and replenish your first aid kit to ensure all items are up-to-date.

Smart Health Gadgets: Heart Rate Monitors, Portable ECGs, and AI-Driven Health Apps

Modern technology has revolutionized medical preparedness. Smart health gadgets provide real-time monitoring and immediate assistance in emergencies.

1. **Heart Rate Monitors & Pulse Oximeters**: Devices like the Garmin or Apple Watch measure heart rate and oxygen saturation, helping detect irregularities early.

2. **Portable ECGs**: Handheld ECG monitors such as KardiaMobile detect arrhythmias and provide instant heart health assessments.
3. **AI-Driven Health Apps**: Mobile apps like Ada, Babylon Health, and WebMD offer symptom analysis, first aid guidance, and emergency contacts.
4. **Smart Wearables**: Devices with fall detection, such as the Apple Watch, alert emergency services in case of accidents.
5. **Telemedicine & Remote Consultation**: Access to virtual healthcare ensures quick medical advice, reducing reliance on in-person visits.

These innovations enhance safety, especially in remote locations or during emergencies.

Using Drones for Medical Supplies Delivery in Remote Areas

Drones have emerged as a game-changer for delivering medical supplies, particularly in hard-to-reach regions.

Benefits of Drone Medical Deliveries:

- **Speed & Efficiency**: Drones bypass traffic and geographical barriers, ensuring rapid delivery of medicine and vaccines.
- **Access to Remote Locations**: Areas with poor infrastructure receive vital supplies without logistical delays.
- **Disaster Response**: Drones provide emergency aid during natural disasters, delivering blood, first aid, and diagnostics.
- **Cost-Effective**: Reduces the need for costly transport infrastructure and human resources.

Real-World Applications:

- **Zipline in Africa**: Delivering blood and medical supplies to rural hospitals in Rwanda and Ghana.
- **Wing (by Alphabet)**: Partnering with healthcare providers to distribute medication and first aid kits.
- **UNICEF's Drone Testing**: Exploring drone deliveries for vaccine transportation in remote areas.

Future Prospects:

- **AI-Powered Drone Navigation**: Enhanced AI algorithms for precision delivery and obstacle avoidance.
- **Autonomous Emergency Response**: AI-driven drones automatically deployed to accident sites.
- **Integration with Wearables**: Real-time health monitoring triggering drone assistance for medical emergencies.

By combining traditional first aid with advanced technology, individuals and communities can be better prepared for medical emergencies, ensuring safety and survival in any situation.

Chapter 10: Off-Grid Living & Long-Term Survival

Setting Up a High-Tech Off-Grid Base

Going off-grid doesn't mean sacrificing modern conveniences. By integrating smart technology with self-sustaining practices, you can build an off-grid base that balances independence with innovation.

Key Components of a High-Tech Off-Grid Base:

1. **Energy Independence:** Utilize a hybrid system combining solar panels, wind turbines, and battery storage.
2. **Water Security:** Rainwater harvesting, filtration systems, and underground cisterns for emergency reserves.
3. **Smart Energy Management:** IoT-enabled monitoring systems to optimize energy consumption and automation.
4. **Communication Systems:** Satellite internet (e.g., Starlink), HAM radio, and long-range walkie-talkies.
5. **Security & Surveillance:** Motion-sensor cameras, perimeter alarms, and drone monitoring.
6. **Food Sustainability:** Advanced hydroponics, permaculture design, and automated greenhouse management.

Solar & Wind Energy for Sustainable Survival

Solar Power:

- Solar panels are the backbone of off-grid energy, providing clean and renewable power.
- Key factors: panel efficiency, battery storage (lithium-ion or lead-acid), and inverter capacity.
- Best practices: Track sun exposure, install at optimal angles, and use a charge controller for efficient energy storage.

Wind Power:

- A viable backup or complementary source of energy, especially in windy regions.
- Small-scale wind turbines can generate power even on cloudy days.
- Consideration: Wind speed consistency, turbine maintenance, and noise reduction.

Hybrid System Optimization:

- Use both solar and wind to balance energy supply.
- Smart energy storage systems ensure power availability during peak and off-peak hours.
- Off-grid inverters and power management systems prevent energy waste.

Building a Bushcraft Smart Home with Rainwater Collection & Hydroponics

A modern off-grid home combines traditional survival skills with contemporary technology.

Bushcraft Meets Smart Living:

- **Natural Materials:** Use locally sourced wood, stone, or cob for construction.
- **Passive Heating & Cooling:** Earth-sheltered designs, geothermal heating, and reflective roofing to maintain temperature.

- **Smart Lighting & Power Usage:** LED lighting, motion-sensing switches, and energy-efficient appliances.

Rainwater Collection System:

1. **Gutters & Filters:** Install high-quality gutter guards and pre-filters to remove debris.
2. **Storage Tanks:** Underground or above-ground tanks made of food-grade plastic or concrete.
3. **Filtration & Purification:** Use multi-stage filters, UV purifiers, and activated carbon to ensure potable water.

Hydroponic Food Production:

- A controlled environment reduces reliance on traditional farming.
- Vertical farming maximizes space efficiency.
- Automated nutrient delivery systems optimize plant growth.
- Best crops: Leafy greens, tomatoes, peppers, and herbs thrive in hydroponic systems.

Best Survival Communities & Online Networks

Surviving long-term off-grid is easier when connected to like-minded individuals. Various online and offline communities exist to share knowledge, trade goods, and provide mutual assistance.

Top Survival Communities & Forums:

1. **Reddit's r/Survival & r/OffGrid** – A vast knowledge base for self-sufficient living and emergency preparedness.
2. **Permies.com** – Focuses on permaculture, homesteading, and sustainable farming.
3. **The Survival Podcast Forum** – A practical hub for discussions on self-reliance and resilience.
4. **Homesteading Today** – Covers topics from renewable energy to food preservation.
5. **Facebook Groups & Discord Servers** – Niche communities for preppers, homesteaders, and alternative living enthusiasts.

Building Local & Offline Networks:

- Join survivalist meetups and workshops.
- Attend off-grid expos and permaculture retreats.
- Form or join local bartering groups to exchange skills, resources, and products.

Going off-grid successfully requires planning, adaptability, and leveraging modern technology to enhance self-sufficiency. By integrating high-tech solutions with time-tested survival skills, you can create a sustainable, resilient lifestyle while remaining connected to a supportive community. Whether you're preparing for an uncertain future or simply seeking freedom from modern dependencies, mastering off-grid living is a rewarding journey toward true independence.

Final Thoughts & Bonus Resources

Mastering bushcraft is about balancing knowledge, skills, and the right tools. Whether you lean towards traditional survival techniques or integrate modern technology, preparation is key. The more you practice, the more self-reliant you become. This guide has equipped you with essential survival strategies—now it's up to you to test them in real-world conditions.

To support your journey, here are additional resources, expert recommendations, and a printable survival cheat sheet to keep handy.

➢ Checklist: High-Tech vs. Traditional Bushcraft Essentials

A well-prepared survivalist understands the benefits of both old-school methods and modern technology. This checklist highlights the must-have essentials from each approach:

Traditional Bushcraft Gear

✓☐ Fixed-blade knife (carbon steel or stainless)
✓☐ Folding saw or hatchet
✓☐ Fire-starting kit (ferro rod, flint & steel, waterproof matches)
✓☐ Cotton bandana (multi-use: filtering water, medical aid, signaling)
✓☐ Waxed canvas tarp or wool blanket
✓☐ Natural fiber cordage (jute twine, plant-based rope)
✓☐ Hand-carved wooden traps & snares
✓☐ Compass and topographic map
✓☐ Hand-powered grain mill & basic foraging tools
✓☐ Leather water pouch or traditional canteen

High-Tech Survival Gear

✓☐ GPS device or offline navigation apps
✓☐ Solar-powered charger & power bank
✓☐ Compact ultralight tent & sleeping system
✓☐ Fireproof, waterproof survival notebook
✓☐ Portable water purifier (UV light or filter pump)
✓☐ LED headlamp & solar lantern
✓☐ Biodegradable energy bars & MREs

✓☐ Satellite communicator (Garmin InReach, Zoleo)
✓☐ Lightweight synthetic thermal clothing
✓☐ Multifunctional survival smartwatch (weather tracking, compass, SOS function)

Whether you prefer the time-tested reliability of traditional bushcraft or the efficiency of modern survival tools, a combination of both ensures greater adaptability in unpredictable situations.

Best Websites, Apps, and Tools for Survivalists

Top Websites for Survival Skills & Bushcraft Knowledge

- **Survival Blog** – A deep well of self-sufficiency and disaster preparedness insights.
- **Bushcraft USA** – A community-driven forum packed with field-tested tips and gear reviews.
- **The Prepared** – A modern approach to prepping with practical advice.
- **Wildwood Survival** – Focused on primitive skills and natural survival techniques.

Must-Have Apps for Survivalists

- **Gaia GPS** – Offline topographic maps for backcountry navigation.
- **Survival Manual** – A comprehensive guide with offline access.
- **Cairn** – Live tracking and safety check-ins for wilderness hikers.
- **Weather Underground** – Real-time weather tracking for extreme conditions.
- **First Aid by American Red Cross** – Emergency medical procedures at your fingertips.

Recommended Bushcraft YouTubers, Podcasts & Experts to Follow

Top Bushcraft YouTubers

- **Ray Mears** – One of the world's foremost bushcraft experts.
- **MCQBushcraft** – Traditional bushcraft techniques, shelter building, and survival skills.

- **Survival Lilly** – Solo survivalist sharing real-world survival scenarios.
- **TA Outdoors** – Bushcraft, shelter-building, and outdoor gear reviews.
- **Joe Robinet** – A mix of solo camping, bushcraft skills, and survival experiments.

Best Bushcraft & Survival Podcasts

- **The Survival Show Podcast** – Expert discussions on gear, training, and strategies.
- **Mind of a Survivor** – Exploring mental resilience in survival situations.
- **The Prepper Broadcasting Network** – Covers everything from homesteading to self-defense.
- **The Survival Podcast** – A mix of modern preparedness and off-grid living tips.

Experts to Follow

- **Dave Canterbury** – Founder of the Pathfinder School, focusing on survival training.
- **Les Stroud ("Survivorman")** – Survival expert known for realistic, solo survival challenges.

- **Cody Lundin** – Primitive survival skills and self-reliance training.
- **Bear Grylls** – Adventurer and survival instructor for extreme situations.

Printable Emergency Survival Cheat Sheet

This survival cheat sheet condenses essential knowledge into an easy-to-carry format. Print it, laminate it, and keep it in your survival kit.

Fire-Making Methods

- Ferro rod + dry tinder
- Flint & steel + char cloth
- Bow drill friction fire
- Solar lens + dry kindling
- Battery + steel wool

Water Purification

- Boil water for 5+ minutes
- Use a portable filter or UV purifier
- Chemical purification (iodine, chlorine tabs)

- Construct a DIY solar still

Navigation Without GPS

- Find North with an analog watch (point hour hand at the sun, halfway between 12 and the hour is South in the Northern Hemisphere)
- Use moss growth (usually on the north side of trees in temperate zones)
- Follow running water downstream to find civilization

Emergency Shelter Options

- **Lean-to** (quick, simple, wind-resistant)
- **Debris Hut** (fully insulated for cold conditions)
- **Tarp A-frame** (fast, waterproof, great for rain protection)
- **Tree Pit Shelter** (snow survival)

Edible vs. Poisonous Plants

- The **Universal Edibility Test**: If unsure, perform a slow, multi-step test (smell, touch, taste in tiny amounts over time).

- Avoid plants with **white or yellow sap, umbrella-shaped flowers, or bitter almonds smell**—these are often toxic.

Signaling for Rescue

- **Three fires in a triangle** = recognized distress signal.
- **Mirror signaling** = direct sunlight toward rescuers.
- **Loud whistle blasts (3x)** = emergency distress signal.

First Aid Basics

- **Control bleeding:** Apply firm pressure and elevate.
- **Treat burns:** Cool with water, do not pop blisters.
- **Shock treatment:** Keep victim warm and lying down.
- **Splint fractures:** Immobilize and use a sturdy support.

This cheat sheet serves as a quick reference in emergencies, ensuring you have vital survival knowledge at your fingertips.

Final Word

Survival is not just about gear—it's about mindset, adaptability, and knowledge. The best way to be prepared is through hands-on experience. Train regularly, test your skills in real scenarios, and always strive to learn more.

Whether you're venturing into the wild for adventure or preparing for unexpected situations, remember: **Stay calm. Stay resourceful. Stay alive.**

Happy survival training!

Table of Contents:

Introduction 5
  What is High-Tech Bushcraft? 5
  Why Blend Classic and Modern Survival Techniques? 6
    1. Redundancy Increases Survival Odds 7
    2. Enhancing Efficiency and Energy Conservation 7
    3. Access to Advanced Safety and Communication 8
    4. Preparedness for a Wide Range of Scenarios 8
    5. Adaptation to Changing Environments 9
  Who is This Guide For? 9
    1. Preppers and Survivalists 9
    2. Adventurers and Explorers 10
    3. Off-Grid Enthusiasts and Homesteaders 10
    4. Military Personnel and Tactical Operators 10
    5. Beginners and Urban Dwellers Seeking Emergency Preparedness 11
  Conclusion 11
Chapter 1: Bushcraft Basics - The Foundation of Survival 12
  Understanding the Core Principles of Bushcraft 12
    1. Shelter 12
    2. Fire 13
    3. Water 13
    4. Food 14
    5. Navigation 14
  Essential Gear: What Every Survivalist Needs 15

Traditional vs. Modern Survival Approaches 16
    Traditional Bushcraft 16
    Modern Survivalism 17
    Which is Better? 17
Conclusion 18
Building Traditional Shelters 19
    Lean-to Shelter 19
    Debris Hut 20
    A-Frame Shelter 21
Modern Shelter Options 22
    Lightweight Tents 22
    Bivy Bags:A bivy bag (short for bivouac sack) is a minimalist shelter alternative to a tent. 22
    Emergency Blankets 23
Smart Survival Clothing 24
    Heated Jackets 24
    Moisture-Wicking Layers 25
    UV Protection Clothing 25
Conclusion 26
Chapter 3: Fire-Making Techniques - Old and New 27
Traditional Fire-Starting Methods 27
    1. Flint & Steel 27
    2. Bow Drill 28
    3. Fire Plough 29
Modern Fire Solutions 29
    1. Plasma Lighters 29

  2. Fire-Starting Gels & Cubes..30

  3. Solar Fire Starters 30

 Best Firewood & Weatherproof Fire Tips..............................31

  Best Firewood Types 31

  Weatherproof Fire Tips...31

Chapter 4: Water Purification - From Primitive to High-Tech
....33

 Finding Water in the Wild: Streams, Plants, and
 Condensation 33

  Streams and Rivers 33

  Rainwater Collection 34

  Dew and Condensation 34

  Plant-Based Water Sources 34

 Traditional Purification Methods (Boiling, Charcoal
 Filtration)...35

  Boiling Water..35

  Charcoal Filtration 36

  Solar Disinfection (SODIS) 36

 Modern Water Filtration & Purifiers 37

  LifeStraw..37

  UV Sterilizers...37

  Reverse Osmosis Bottles 38

 Conclusion 39

Chapter 5: High-Tech Navigation & Tracking.............................40

 Using the Sun, Stars, and Landmarks 40

  The Sun..41

  The Stars 41

Landmarks 42

Compasses vs. GPS: When to Use Which 42

    Compass Navigation 42

    GPS Navigation 43

Best Survival Navigation Apps 43

Modern smartphones and handheld GPS devices have revolutionized outdoor navigation. Here are some of the best survival navigation apps available: 44

    Gaia GPS 44

    AllTrails 44

    Google Maps (Offline Mode) 44

    ViewRanger 45

    onX Hunt 45

Drones for Scouting & Safety 45

    Best Drone Models for Navigation & Safety 46

    How to Use Drones in the Wild 46

    Drone Usage Tips 47

Conclusion 47

Chapter 6: Food & Foraging in the Digital Age 48

Wild Edibles Identification: Traditional Knowledge 48

Foraging Apps & AI-Powered Plant Identification 49

Hunting & Fishing Gadgets: Thermal Scopes, Fish Finders, and More 50

    Hunting Technology 51

    Fishing Technology 51

DIY Survival Food: Freeze-Drying, Solar Dehydration, and Smart Preservation 52

  Freeze-Drying 52

  Solar Dehydration 53

  Smart Preservation Techniques 53

  Building a Sustainable Food Strategy 54

 Conclusion 55

  Best Multi-Tools & Smart Knives 56

  Solar Chargers & Power Banks for Off-Grid Energy 58

  Ham Radios, Satellite Phones & Emergency Beacons ... 60

  3D-Printed Survival Tools: Customizing Your Own Gear
.... 62

  Conclusion 64

Chapter 8: Self-Defense & Security in the Wild 65

 Traditional Self-Defense: Spears, Traps, and Primitive
Weapons 65

  Spears 66

  Traps 66

  Primitive Weapons 67

 Modern Survival Weapons: Compact Crossbows, Tactical
Pens, and Pepper Spray 67

  Compact Crossbows 67

  Tactical Pens 68

  Pepper Spray 68

 Best Motion Sensors & Perimeter Alarms for Campsites . 69

  Motion Sensors 69

  Perimeter Alarms 70

  Recommended Products 70

 Final Thoughts 71

Chapter 9: Medical Preparedness - Traditional & Tech-Driven 72

Basic Wilderness First Aid Skills 72

Survival First Aid Kits: What to Pack 73

Basic Medical Supplies: 74

Medications: 74

Advanced Supplies: 74

Survival Tools: 75

Smart Health Gadgets: Heart Rate Monitors, Portable ECGs, and AI-Driven Health Apps 75

Using Drones for Medical Supplies Delivery in Remote Areas 76

Benefits of Drone Medical Deliveries: 77

Real-World Applications: 77

Future Prospects: 78

Setting Up a High-Tech Off-Grid Base 78

Key Components of a High-Tech Off-Grid Base: 79

Solar & Wind Energy for Sustainable Survival 80

Building a Bushcraft Smart Home with Rainwater Collection & Hydroponics 81

Bushcraft Meets Smart Living: 81

Rainwater Collection System: 82

Hydroponic Food Production: 82

Best Survival Communities & Online Networks 83

Top Survival Communities & Forums: 83

Building Local & Offline Networks: 84

Final Thoughts & Bonus Resources 85

99

- Checklist: High-Tech vs. Traditional Bushcraft Essentials 85

Best Websites, Apps, and Tools for Survivalists 87

Recommended Bushcraft YouTubers, Podcasts & Experts to Follow 88

Printable Emergency Survival Cheat Sheet 90

Final Word 93

Made in the USA
Columbia, SC
20 June 2025